The Power *of* Crying Out

The Secret to Overcoming Fear

BILL GOTHARD

God "commandeth, and raiseth the stormy wind, which lifteth up the waves thereof. They mount up to the heaven, they go down again to the depths: their soul is melted because of trouble. . . .

Then they cry unto the LORD in their trouble,

and he bringeth them out of their distresses. He maketh the storm a calm, so that the waves thereof are still." PSALM 107:25–29

Phillip Zhang

Institute in Basic Life Principles
Oak Brook, Illinois

Published by the Institute in Basic Life Principles, Inc.
Box One
Oak Brook, IL 60522-3001
Tel: 630-323-9800
Fax: 630-323-7271
www.iblp.org

The Institute in Basic Life Principles is a Biblically based, not-for-profit, nonsectarian training and service organization dedicated to serving families, youth, and leaders worldwide, through training in Biblical principles that bring true success in life.

International Standard Book Number: 0-916888-21-5

Printed in the United States of America
Second Edition
01 02 03 04 05 06 — 10 9 8 7 6 5 4 3 2 1

Table
of Contents

Introduction

It was only a few years ago that I began to comprehend the significance of crying out to God. What has been most amazing to me is that He will arrange or allow circumstances to arise that have no solution and then do nothing to remove the problem until I cry out—not one second sooner!

Each situation seems so hopeless, and a cry appears to be so futile. Yet this is precisely the setting that God wants in order to demonstrate His loving care for us and His powerful hand of protection over us.

Sometimes a cry will bring freedom from emotional bondage; in other cases, God will give clear direction on what to do. In still other situations, He will cause others to provide just the right assistance or resources that are needed.

In every circumstance, the need to cry out is a humbling reminder of my total inability to accomplish anything significant for God, and the result of crying out is a wonderful demonstration of His supernatural power and provision!

I encourage you to carefully read this book and then write out your own experiences of crying out in the pages that are provided for this purpose.

If you would like to share a remarkable experience with others, please send it to me, so that we can find the best way to pass it on to others and thereby glorify God. His promise is certainly true, "Call unto me, and I will answer thee, and shew thee great and mighty things, which thou knowest not."[1]

Bill Gothard
President
Institute in Basic Life Principles

Chapter 1

Eyewitness Accounts of the Power of Crying Out to God

How the Cry of a Victim Was More Powerful Than the Gun of a Robber

This account appeared in The Dallas Morning News *on October 28, 2001, in an article titled "Gunman faces off with prayer's power" by columnist Steve Blow.*

Sherman Jackson was a little late for the share service at his church on a recent Sunday night.

But that was OK. He had quite a story to share once he got there.

Sherman, 36, and his 7-year-old daughter, Alexa, had stopped for gas on their way to church. This was on Northwest Highway, where Garland and Mesquite and Dallas all meet.

As they were about to drive away, a 30-ish fellow walked up. "Hey, man, I need your help," he said. "Could you please help me jump-start my car? I'll pay you to help me."

Sherman fretted a moment about being late for church. Then he chided himself for thinking of that over helping someone.

So he invited the fellow to get in the front seat. Alexa was in back. And they drove off.

They hadn't gone far when the man reached into his pocket. "I thought he was trying to get out some change to pay me for helping him," Sherman said. But no.

"He pulled out a revolver with his right hand and placed his left hand on my shoulder. He pointed the revolver into my rib cage and said, "OK, man, this is for real. You give me all of your money right now, or I'm going to unload this gun on you."

Sherman was terrified, of course. And mad at himself for putting his daughter in danger.

"OK, look, here's all I have on me," he said, pulling out his money clip. "Take it all."

But the robber didn't believe him. "That's not all. Give it all to me," he said, shoving the gun harder into Sherman's ribs.

Sherman, a Garland insurance agent, keeps Gideon Bibles in his car with a dollar bill tucked in each one. He gives them to the homeless. The gunman spotted one of those bills sticking out and began to scream at Sherman: "You lied to me! There is more money here."

Something came over Sherman just then, and he began to pray out loud. "Father in heaven, hear my cry and deliver me from this present evil . . ."

He felt a sudden calm. "I lost all consciousness of concern and worry," he said. "A boldness took over."

He slowed the car and began to make a U-turn. The gunman screamed, "What are you doing?"

"This car is being turned around," Sherman replied, "and I am not taking orders from you anymore."

The man put the gun against Sherman's chest. "You don't get it, man. You mean nothing to me. I'll pull this trigger."

"No, you don't understand," Sherman cut him off. "Greater is he that is in me than he that is in the world. My Jesus is stronger than your gun."

He could see the gunman tug on the trigger. The hammer drew back. But Sherman didn't flinch. He pulled over and stopped.

"I want to tell you about Jesus," he said to the gunman.

The man wavered a moment, lowered his gun, and then dropped his head. When he looked up, he was crying. "I'm so sorry, man. I'm so, so sorry," he said. "I was going to shoot you."

"Don't worry about it. I forgive you," Sherman said. And then he began to tell the man about new life through belief in Jesus.

Sherman urged the man to go on to church with him, but he declined. He asked Sherman to drive him to his car at a store.

Along the way, the man began to tell Sherman about all his problems. He said his name was Mike and reached out to shake Sherman's hand. Sherman continued talking to him about starting life anew with God.

As they neared the grocery, Sherman said, "And by the way, Mike, I want my money clip back."

"Do what?!" Mike exclaimed. But then he meekly handed it over.

"And," Sherman went on, "you are keeping this New Testament, and you are going to read it like you never read anything else before. And I'm going to be praying for you, Mike, that God will come into your life."

They pulled alongside Mike's car. "He got out," Sherman said, "with the revolver in one hand, the Bible in the other hand, and tears in his eyes."

And Sherman drove on to church.

Reprinted with permission of The Dallas Morning News

Sherman has given a more detailed account of this event and continues to marvel at the amazing peace and boldness that came over him as soon as he cried out to the Lord. He has since learned that his assailant actually robbed about fifteen other people. No one resisted him and no one else got their money back.

Local police who now know who the robber is have assured Sherman that he is very fortunate to be alive; and for those who doubted the validity of Sherman's story, the columnist came out with a follow-up several days later.

The following article appeared in the November 2, 2001, edition of *The Dallas Morning News*, in an article titled "Remorseful bandit back on sinful path."

When last we left "Mike" the remorseful bandit, he was standing in a grocery parking lot with a Bible in one hand and a gun in the other.

It wasn't clear then which grip was tighter.

But alas, it seems the gun won.

In Sunday's column, I told you about Sherman Jackson's amazing encounter on the way to church a few weeks ago.

The Garland man basically prayed his way out of a robbery—and left the teary-eyed bandit clutching a Bible instead of Sherman's money clip.

Lots of you said you loved that story. Thank you. And a few said they just flat didn't believe it. A little too perfect, they said.

Well, maybe their cynical hearts will be warmed to know that the bandit apparently returned to his ways.

Mike's attempted holdup of Sherman on Sunday evening of Oct. 7 was one in a rash of 15 or so nearly identical robberies in the area around Northwest Highway and LBJ Freeway.

Garland police Detective W. A. Ellstrom noticed that the robberies did stop in the week after Sherman's encounter, so perhaps that Bible wasn't ditched immediately.

But the detective said the robberies fit the classic pattern of a drug addict, so good intentions may have crumbled in the face of drug cravings.

Some readers criticized Sherman for not reporting the crime. Actually, he tried. He called police that night, but when he said no money was taken and no one was hurt, he was told to call another number at a later time.

"There didn't seem to be a lot of interest, so I just never called back," he said.

But now he's working closely with Garland police, helping on a composite sketch of the suspect.

I asked Sherman about his attitude toward the robber now. "It's the same as before," he said. "I'll continue praying for him. And I hope he gets caught."

Reprinted with permission of The Dallas Morning News

The Cry That Solved the Crime When Police Said a Case Was Hopeless

The owner of a plumbing company in the Chicago area bought a large truck to hold all the tools he needed for his jobs. Thus, he had a mobile plumbing shop.

One day he drove his truck to a local store to take care of a business matter. He would be gone for only a few minutes, so he left the key in the ignition. When he returned, the truck was gone.

He was stunned and called the police. They informed him that car thieves regularly circled the area, looking for just such opportunities to steal a vehicle. The policeman told him, "If we cannot locate your truck in an hour, you might as well forget about it. The thieves are well organized and quickly dispose of what they steal."

At that point, the owner asked some friends to pray. On October 13, 2000, these friends cried out to God on his behalf. Their cry was simple: "Abba, Father, cause the thief to repent and return the truck."

Three days later, the owner received a phone call from someone in Chicago, saying, "Come and get your truck." He went to the address that he was given, and there it was! It was still intact—checks and job orders were still in the truck, but many of the tools were missing.

A few days later, he went to a flea market and spotted some of his missing tools. After proving that they were his, he was able to recover them. During the three days that the truck was missing, a widow of a plumber heard about his plight and gave him all her husband's tools. Another friend also gave him many tools and copper fittings.

This experience produced a tremendous joy in him and in all his friends who had cried out to God. Most of all, it drew him closer to the Lord and to the reality of God's promise in Psalm 50:15: "And call upon me in the day of trouble: I will deliver thee, and thou shalt glorify me."[1]

How Two Terrifying Moments Proved the Power of the Right Cry

A father was driving on a southern Illinois highway to visit his son at the university. It was a cold, wintry day, and suddenly, his vehicle began spinning out of control on a patch of ice he had not seen. He felt helpless as he headed for the ditch, expecting damage and injury. God could have allowed him to see the ice, or He could have kept the vehicle on the road. So why did God let this happen?

When the father whose car was out of control realized his danger, he cried out, "O God, deliver me!" Just then it was like a hand put the car back on the road heading in the right direction. He rejoiced in this deliverance and continued driving. About twenty minutes later, he hit yet another patch of ice and spun out of control. This time he simply said, "Oh, no!" and continued on into the ditch.

How the Heart of a Rebellious Daughter Was Won by the Cry of Her Mother

A mother in Melbourne, Australia, was shocked and grieved when her sixteen-year-old daughter ran off with an older boy. This boy had stolen her daughter's affections and convinced her to reject her family and come with him. The mother had been trying to protect her daughter from wrong friendships and damaging decisions, and now she felt like a failure. Why did God let this happen?

This mother knew that she could turn to no one for help, so she went into a room, putting a towel over her mouth to muffle the sound. Then with all of her strength she cried out, "O God, deliver my daughter from this boy!" The next day someone gave her a flyer announcing the first Basic Seminar in Melbourne, Australia. Her husband was also given a flyer. They decided to go, and asked their daughter to attend. She agreed.

On Monday night, she liked the session so much that she asked her boyfriend to go with her the next night. He came, and the following night he became so convicted about what he had done that he repented and also asked both the Lord and the girl's parents to forgive him. The boy and the girl agreed to separate from each other so that each one could grow in faith in the Lord and rebuild family relationships.

How a Cry Saved a Comfortable Farmer From Being Crushed to Death

A farmer in Michigan became very prosperous, so he rewarded himself with the most efficient, high-powered tractor he could buy. One day he was using it with a conveyor belt to haul his crops to the top of the barn. Suddenly, his sleeve got caught in the mechanism, and he was jerked into the path of the large wheel. He realized that in a few seconds he would be crushed to death, as was a neighbor in a similar accident a few weeks before.

He cried out in a loud voice, "O God, save me!" and the engine suddenly stalled. A farmhand ran out to rescue him, and together they realized that only God could have stopped that engine, since there was no mechanical reason for this happening.

As the farmer publicly gave this report, he also acknowledged that before that experience, he did not feel that he needed the Lord because things were going so well for him. Now he realizes that every day is a gift from the Lord. He knows that he is "a dead man on furlough."

How the Prediction of Doctors in Russia Was Reversed by a Cry

In September 2001, a nineteen-year-old Russian boy named Dima dived into a shallow river. He broke his neck and his back in two places, puncturing a lung and receiving other internal injuries. The nearest hospital was forty miles away.

When he finally arrived at the hospital, the best doctors in Moscow were waiting for him because of the influence of his grandmother, who is a government official. After examining Dima, they all concluded that there was no way that he could survive.

When our staff learned about this incident, we realized that it would be a wonderful opportunity for God to show His power. Therefore, we cried out, "O God, deliver Dima from death and raise him up for Your glory."

We also contacted prison chaplains and urged that the alumni of Basic Seminars in the prisons also cry out for Dima. They did this. A week later, we talked with Dima's grandmother, who thanked us for crying out and announced that the doctors had now reversed their prognosis, stating that Dima would live. He is receiving therapy and learning to use his hands and arms.

How a Baby in Distress Was Delivered by a Fervent Cry

The wife of one of our staff members was in the process of delivering a baby. However, the baby was in the wrong position and after several hours of labor, there was no more sign of a heartbeat. This meant an automatic c-section and the possibility of a dead child. I gathered six or seven staff members together, and we cried out for this mother and baby.

The cry was based on the promise, "Call upon me in the day of trouble, and I will deliver thee, and thou shalt glorify me."[2] In unison, we cried out, "O God, this is a day of trouble. Deliver this baby quickly in good health!" Within twenty minutes, the baby was delivered in good health without a c-section.

How a Pharmacist Used a Cry to Save His Marriage and His Patient's Sight

In December of 1999, a woman came into a pharmacy with a prescription from her eye doctor. The pharmacist filled the prescription. However, he made a dispensing error and filled the prescription incorrectly. As she applied it to her eye, the damage began. Her eyes burned and swelled. She finally returned to her eye doctor. He saw what had happened and was shocked. He told her she was using the wrong medication.

When she told the pharmacist what he had done, he was alarmed, especially when he saw the condition of her eyes. He then gave her the right medication and hoped that it would help. However, her condition worsened. Through January, February, March, and April she periodically visited the pharmacist and showed him her deteriorating condition. By April the doctors could not be sure that she would ever improve.

The desperate pharmacist was very aware of the moral and legal liability of his error, so he set aside a weekend to seek the Lord and pray for her healing. During this important time, God reminded him of an area of sensual bondage in his life. He knew God was telling him to confess it to his wife and to forsake it. This would be the most humbling thing he would ever do.

May 31 was "D-day" (death to pride) for this pharmacist. He told his wife of his secret sin and was shocked at what happened. She informed him that because of his lack of affection, she had decided to leave him with their three children. His confession caused her to change her mind and purpose to work at making the marriage successful.

The following day, the woman with the eye infection came to see him. She was delighted and amazed because healing was now coming to her eye!

How the Power of a Cry Was Greater Than the Push of a Thief

"As I was getting out of my car one afternoon at a Basic Seminar, a young man approached me and asked what convention was going on. I began to tell him it was a Basic Youth Conflicts Seminar, but before I could say any more, he pulled a revolver out of his pocket and started to push me into my car. He said, 'You're not going anywhere. Get back into the car.'

"Immediately, the Holy Spirit brought to my mind the principle of calling out loud to God, and I cried out, 'O God, help me! Please Lord Jesus, deliver me!' God was faithful to His promise. The man backed off as if another power was pushing him away, and he fled."

How Crying Out to God Accomplished What Screams Failed to Do

"I went to a self-service car wash, which I considered to be a safe place. It was very well-lit and there were other businesses on the same block. I had just started washing the car when a man came from behind me and grabbed me around the neck. He started pulling me toward a vacant lot behind the car wash.

"I began screaming and yelling. Another man came up and grabbed my feet. I continued screaming for help. They continued dragging me. But then I cried out, 'In the name of Jesus Christ, put me down!' They instantly dropped me and ran away."

Why a Cry Is So Effective in Responding to an Attack

By crying out to God, we are asking Him to overcome the power of evil, which only He can do because He is over all principalities and powers. And Scripture states, "We wrestle not against flesh and blood, but against principalities, against powers, against the rulers of the darkness of this world, against spiritual wickedness in high places."[3]

A further reason for the effectiveness of a cry is that most wickedness is carried out by those who have no awareness of the presence of God and, therefore, no fear of Him. However, when the intended victim cries out for God to deliver him from an evil person, the awareness of God is suddenly present. As Scripture states, "By the fear of the LORD men depart from evil."[4]

Chapter 2

How a Violent Storm Gives Three Vital Lessons on Crying Out

One day, Jesus told His disciples to get into their boat and sail to the other side of the Sea of Galilee. This request was significant because Jesus knew then that it would be impossible for them to carry out His command. He knew that a violent storm was going to engulf their boat and that treacherous winds and waves would overwhelm them.

With this knowledge, He climbed into the boat with them, found a comfortable spot in the bow, and fell fast asleep. Several disciples were seasoned fishermen, so when they observed dark clouds gathering on the horizon and saw the whitecaps across the water, they assumed that it would be just another storm.

Soon, however, they realized that this was no ordinary storm. The violent wind lashed their faces with the surf, and angry waves crested and crashed over their boat, filling it with water. Yet they struggled on with all their might.

Finally, they concluded that it was no longer a matter of reaching the opposite shore—it was a matter of survival. They fully expected to perish. It was only then that they cried out to the Lord: "Master, save us lest we perish!" And it was only then that Jesus acted to still the storm.[1]

Lesson Number One

The commands that Jesus gives sound achievable until we try to carry them out.

One of Jesus' commands is, "Love your enemies." This sounds a bit difficult, yet possible, until we put faces on our enemies. When our "enemy" turns out to be a father who is always angry, harsh, and unloving, or a mother who is always nagging and untrusting, or siblings who are constant irritations, then waves of angry emotions and howling winds of adverse circumstances make this command a practical impossibility.

We forget about loving them and look around for some "nicer" enemies who are easier to love—enemies whom we do not have to live with and whom we have never met. However, the enemies to whom Jesus was referring are the very ones He allows in our lives and from whom we cannot get away, just like the monstrous waves that overwhelmed the disciples in their boat.

Jesus knew about these enemies when He said to His disciples, "A man's foes shall be they of his own household."[2] David also experienced unexpected adversity from those he never imagined would be his enemies. He wrote, "It was not an enemy that reproached me; then I could have borne it: neither was it he that hated me that did magnify himself against me; then I would have hid myself from him: But it was thou, a man mine equal, my guide, and mine acquaintance. We took sweet counsel together, and walked unto the house of God in company."[3]

A wife will exclaim, "What about a husband who is violating his marriage vows and is abusive to the children?" A husband will ask, "What about a wife who is unloving and always angry at the children?" Children will ask, "What about parents whom you can never please?" These are the storms that cause marriages and families to sink, and these are precisely the times that there is no other solution but to cry out to God.

Lesson Number Two

Jesus does nothing to still our storms until we cry out to Him.

Most people find it hard to cry out for help, especially men. We want to be self-sufficient. We are taught to think positively and to keep reminding ourselves that we can do it. We vicariously relive dramas of those who tenaciously endured in the face of insurmountable odds.

If you want an almost-automatic response of laughter, just talk about the different responses of men and women who are lost while driving on a highway. A woman will usually look for the nearest gas station to ask for directions, but a man will drive on, determined to find his way. It usually takes an unsolvable crisis to get a man to cry out for help, and that is precisely why God creates the crises of life.

God's ways of life are usually opposite our ways of reasoning. We think we must be strong to survive. God says that we must recognize our weakness in order to experience His strength. Thus, the Apostle Paul wrote, "When I am weak, then am I strong."[4] There is no better way to express our weakness than to cry out to God for deliverance.

The Storms of Lustful Passions

Many men live with violent storms of anger and lust. They are addicted to pornography and other forms of immorality. They have been overwhelmed with periodic tidal waves of mental and physical passions. On a June morning in a Knoxville, Tennessee, convention center, several thousand men dealt with this situation by getting on their knees and in one loud voice crying out, "Abba, Father, in the name of Jesus, deliver me from anger and lust."

The effectiveness of that cry is reported in the following letter, written by one of the men a few months later.

> The men's sessions were especially important to me when we covered the material on conquering the five giants each of us must face. Two of the giants, anger and lust, had been particularly devastating in my life, affecting my relationships with people that were closest to me.
>
> That Friday as we all knelt in the auditorium, I was overwhelmed by my absolute helplessness to

overcome the least little habit—much less a great giant that had dominated so much of my life. I broke down in tears as the two or three thousand men there at the convention center began crying out to God for deliverance and victory. With all my heart (in great hopelessness of my own abilities) I cried out to Him, "Abba, Father . . . Daddy!"

Even now as I write this, I am overcome with emotion. I walked away from there and I felt no immediate change. But as I returned home something was different. There was a measurable decrease in the influence of temptation. There was a new freedom and feeling of victory for the first time in my life. Now when I am tempted I can actually think, "I am not afraid!" and I calmly praise the Lord because He hath given me the victory this day! My heart is overwhelmed with joy. I've been freed from that prison. — *A grateful father from Indiana*

I have been amazed at how just one cry will bring immediate results, but we should not always expect this to be the case. Sometimes we need to cry day and night. When Jesus taught His disciples to cry out, He used the example of a widow pleading with an unjust judge for help. At first the judge would not respond, but then he thought to himself, "Though I fear not God, nor regard man; Yet because this widow troubleth me, I will avenge her, lest by her continual coming she weary me.

"And the Lord said, Hear what the unjust judge saith. And shall not God avenge his own elect, which cry day and night unto him, though he bear long with them? I tell you that he will avenge them speedily."[5]

Sometimes a delay is based on God's timing to get the greatest glory, as in the Biblical account of Lazarus being raised from the dead, and sometimes it is because of our failure to qualify for deliverance.

It is amazing that when the wind and the waves over-whelmed the disciples, Jesus did not rise up from His sleep in the boat and just calm the storm. He waited for the disciples to cry out for help. This is His pattern and program to keep us in close fellowship with Him and His power. He knows that we do not do well with ease and prosperity. We tend to become independent and believe that we can run our own lives. We either tell Him that we do not need Him, or we live as if this were the case.

He will allow us to indulge in such self-delusions and may even give us the desires of our hearts with "leanness" to our souls, but then problems that we think will clear up get worse and eventually go beyond our ability to handle. God designed these "storms" to bring us back to fellowship with Him, but Satan will try to use them to get us to become angry and bitter. Thus, the same situations that cause us to get bitter are the very circumstances that God designed to show us His power and love. He just waits for us to cry out.

One of my favorite examples of no response from God until I cried out took place at our Northwoods Conference Center in 1999. The young men in our ALERT (Air Land Emergency Resource Team) program were preparing for a father-son camp-out. They were instructed to cut down some midsized trees to be used for benches in an outdoor amphitheater.

With over two thousand acres in the middle of the Ottawa National Forest, there was no lack of trees. However, the fellows happened to take a number of trees from a neighbor's property. The property line was unmarked and our property surrounded his on three sides, so their mistake was understandable. However, when we called the neighbor and apologized with an offer to pay him for the trees that were cut, he accused us of intentionally cutting down the trees and demanded $7,000.00 dollars.

We knew the trees were nowhere near this value, so we called in a log evaluater who estimated that, at most, the price would be about $860.00. We then called our neighbor and offered him almost $1,400.00. He became even more obstinate, claiming that the young men knowingly trespassed on his property, and restated his demand for $7,000.00 or he would take us to court. He gave us a deadline for the payment.

On the day of the deadline, I reviewed our situation. The more I looked at the problem, the more impossible it seemed. In this ministry, every dollar is valuable. To pay $7,000.00 was unthinkable. On the other hand, we were guilty, and going to court would consume valuable time, thousands of dollars in lawyers' fees, and even greater outrage from our neighbor. Here was a situation where there was no good solution for us.

I knew I had to call the man, but what should I say to him? God reminded me that this was a time to cry out. I got on my face before the Lord and cried out in a loud voice, "O Lord, Abba, Father, deliver us from this situation!"

As soon as I finished my cry, two words clearly came to my mind. At first, I did not understand their significance, so I repeated them two or three times in my mind: "Buy it! Buy it? Oh, buy the land!"

I then called the neighbor. As soon as he realized who I was, he immediately started rehearsing the situation. I assured him we would do what was right. I then asked him when he obtained the land. He said, "In 1952." I asked him what his purpose was in getting it. He said, "We got it for an investment." I inquired, "Have you ever thought about selling it?" He said, "For the right price." I asked, "What is the right price?" He replied, "Fifteen thousand dollars."

This was amazing! I tried to remain calm. Property with pine and hardwoods with a stream at the back and a road at the front for only $8,000.00 more than he wanted for the trees we had cut down? I told him I would check on some things and call him right back.

I hung up the phone and checked with myself. I realized that the board of directors had given me prior authorization for purchases up to that amount. Therefore, I quickly called the neighbor back and told him, "We will buy your property at your price." He said, "Fine." Then I added, "This will solve our whole problem, won't it?" He replied, "It certainly will!" He then contacted our attorney, and the sale was finalized.

At a later date, we discovered that what we thought was an easement across the property was actually property owned by the county. Since the title company assured us that it was just an easement, they compensated for their error by giving us $5,000.00.

Thus, for $3,000.00 more than the neighbor originally wanted for the trees, we purchased his entire tract of beautiful Northwoods property.

I am confident that it never would have been on my mind to buy the property had I not cried out to God in what was a hopeless situation.

Lesson Number Three

The storms that God stirs up are designed to bring glory to Him.

The account of the disciples in the storm is strikingly similar to a Psalm that David wrote hundreds of years earlier. It not only describes the wind and the waves, but explains the purpose for which this and other conflicts arise.

> They that go down to the sea in ships, that do business in great waters; These see the works of the LORD, and his wonders in the deep. For he commandeth, and raiseth the stormy wind, which lifteth up the waves thereof. They mount up to the heaven, they go down again to the depths: their soul is melted because of trouble. They reel to and fro, and stagger like a drunken man, and are at their wit's end.
>
> Then they cry unto the LORD in their trouble, and he bringeth them out of their distresses. He maketh the storm a calm, so that the waves thereof are still. Then are they glad because they be quiet; so he bringeth them unto their desired haven.

Oh that men would praise the LORD for his goodness, and for his wonderful works to the children of men! Let them exalt him also in the congregation of the people, and praise him in the assembly of the elders.[6]

This Psalm describes three other hopeless situations that forced individuals to cry out to God. Each cry brought deliverance along with the refrain, "O that men would praise the Lord for his goodness, and for his wonderful works to the children of men!"

The relationship between our trials, the need to cry out, and God's glory is all explained in Scripture: "Call upon me in the day of trouble: I will deliver thee, and thou shalt glorify me."[7]

Any one of the examples of crying out given in the first chapter could have been avoided by the Lord's protection because all power is given to Him in heaven and on earth, but then there would be no story that would illustrate the power of God and His loving care for His people.

When a tragedy happens, we tend to blame God or wonder why He let it happen. We fail to realize that the very nature of God is love, but love requires us to have a free choice in a matter, and a free choice means that our wrong choices will produce devastating consequences for us and our descendants. God will not overrule our will, but He will do all that He can to motivate us to choose His will and restore the type of fellowship that Adam and Eve originally enjoyed with Him so that He can continue walking and talking with us throughout eternity.

Chapter 3

Why a Cry Is Usually More Powerful Than a Prayer

A teenager was quite open about the fact that he did not believe in God. When questioned about his reasons, he stated, "Our family was going through a very hard time, and I prayed that God would help us—but nothing happened. So I just don't believe that there is a God."

Another teenager went through similar trials in her family. Her father had been out of work for over a year. Every day their family prayed that there would be some response to the many resumés that he had sent out—but nothing happened.

The daughter discussed the problem with a counselor and then called home to give her father some ideas for employment. Her father carefully explained why each suggestion would not work. Following that call, all her hopes for a solution vanished.

Later that day, she walked out to a quiet place and cried out, "O God, deliver my father from unemployment." The next day, her mother called and excitedly reported that her father had been given an excellent job and would start work immediately.

Another testimony of resolving family pressures through a cry came in the following report.

Two years ago, I made some very foolish financial decisions. As a result, I and my family were in trouble! Shortly after this, I attended my first Basic Seminar. There I had my first exposure to the teaching on crying out.

When I got home, I rejected it as something that did not apply to my situation. God increased the pressure on me and my family, and we finally faced bankruptcy.

I was $20,000 in debt with unsecured loans. For two years I had been trying to sell some land to cover the debt, but I couldn't even get a phone call of interest. I tried realtor after realtor without success. Finally, in desperation, I walked into the woods and cried, "O God!" That's all that came out. My voice failed as emotion flooded me, and I groaned in my spirit.

The next day, a couple told my wife that they had heard we had land for sale. Within twenty-four hours of crying out, we had an agreement to sell the land for $20,000. Praise God! We are now debt-free and living by God's financial principles.

The second time I cried out involved another kind of personal bondage. I have long been held captive by lust. In the third grade, while walking home from school, I picked up what looked like a comic book. It was my first exposure to pornography. My young heart was captured.

Lust nearly ruined my marriage on numerous occasions. I truly wanted to be free from it and confessed it many times to God. I even sought help from Christian counselors.

In May 2001, your message on crying out was given at our men's meeting. For two more weeks I struggled with lust. Finally on the way to work, I stopped the car and cried out to God for deliverance from lust. God was faithful, and the bondage has been broken.

The Potential of Power With God

For many years I was aware of my inadequate prayer life. I would read biographies of great Christians and marvel at the hours they spent in prayer. I would always be convicted when I read the question and command that Jesus gave Peter in the garden: "What, could ye not watch with me one hour? Watch and pray, that ye enter not into temptation." The next words of Jesus would give me a little comfort. "The spirit indeed is willing, but the flesh is weak."[1] Then three years ago, I followed the example of the disciples and asked, "Lord, teach me to pray."

He directed my attention to the prophet Elijah who had power with God. "Elias was a man subject to like passions as we are, and he prayed earnestly that it might not rain: and it rained not on the earth by the space of three years and six months. And he prayed again, and the heaven gave rain, and the earth brought forth her fruit."[2] One word stood out to me with significance—the word *earnestly*.

The Requirements of Fervency

James introduces the account of Elijah's prayer with the statement, "The effectual fervent prayer of a righteous man availeth much."[3] *Availeth much* literally means, "makes much power available."

The phrase *effectual fervent* is one Greek word, *energeo*. It has the same roots as our English word *energy*. The Apostle Paul uses this word to describe the strivings that he exercised through the power of God within him. "Whereunto I also labour, striving according to his working [*energeia*], which worketh [*energeo*] in me mightily."[4]

The fact is that much of our prayer lacks the kind of fervency that God requires for effective results. On the other hand, when a person cries out to God as his last hope for deliverance, provision, or protection, we can be quite certain that it will be fervent.

How a Desperate Cry Accomplished
What No Diet Had Been Able to Do

Ken Pierpont knew that self-control was a good character quality. He even gave sermons on the subject because he is a minister. However, it was quite obvious to his congregation and to his doctor that he had not learned this quality.

One day he attended a birthday party for his mother-in-law. One of the birthday gifts was a floor scale. The party guests took turns stepping on the scale to weigh themselves. When Ken stood on the scale, it read "Error." He took things out of his pockets and took off his shoes and belt. Finally, it registered 300 pounds!

Ken had tried many different weight-loss programs and diets to solve his problem, but nothing worked for him. He even fasted for forty days and lost about forty pounds, but a few weeks later, the weight was back on. He read books on nutrition and tried to change his eating habits, but soon he slipped back into his old ways. One morning, Ken looked in the mirror and realized that all his efforts were hopeless and there was only one thing left to do, and that was to cry out to God. With great sincerity, he cried out, "O God, deliver me from being overweight and give me self-control." Since that day in June of 2000, Ken had self-control for every meal until he reached his ideal weight of 195 pounds. Within six months, he had lost one hundred pounds. With God's help, he has been able to stay at his healthy weight ever since then.

You can get a firsthand report of Ken's experience by checking his Web site at www.kenpierpont.com.

The Power of Crying Out in One Accord

A further insight into effective prayer is given in the Acts account of the first-century Church. "And when they had prayed, the place was shaken where they were assembled together."[5] Four times in the first five chapters of Acts we are told that the disciples were in "one accord."[6] When they prayed, "they lifted up their voice to God with one accord."

When an entire group cries out in right relationship with the Lord and with each other, they are in one accord, and powerful results take place. The difference between the prayer we commonly experience in a prayer meeting and one-accord crying out that took place in the first-century Church is analogous to the difference between diffused light and a laser beam.

When one person leads a group in prayer, those who listen are often distracted by other thoughts and concerns. However, when the entire group focuses on an urgent need and cries out in unison, there is little chance of distraction.

In January 2001, Pastor Jerry Wells and the congregation of Western Hills Church in Oklahoma City established a new order of service. It is based on the order given for the first-century Church.[7] They begin with the message; then various members give planned and spontaneous testimonies to confirm the message. This is followed by public confessions and communion, along with appropriate songs.

At the conclusion of communion, the pastor announces that anyone who will not be able to concentrate during his time of prayer and crying out or who has other responsibilities can leave. Because the people do not want to miss the mighty working of God, only about 20 percent leave.

After beginning this new schedule, one of their elders asked that they cry out for his physical condition. He had contracted a virus that damaged his ability to walk. Seventeen different doctors had not been able to help him. The entire congregation cried out in unison, "O Lord, deliver our elder from this infirmity." At the end of the prayer time, the elder sensed new strength surging through his legs. He walked forward and gave a public testimony of God's healing power. This caused the entire church and all who knew him to glorify God.

Distinguishing Prayer From Crying Out

For most of my life, I assumed that crying out was simply synonymous with prayer; however, when I saw the specific purposes and potential for crying out, I was amazed to see how these two activities are defined and used in Scripture. One of the clearest indications that they are two distinct and separate responses comes from the passages where both prayer and crying out are mentioned together. The following passages are examples.

- "Attend unto my **cry**, give ear unto my **prayer**."[8]
- "Hear my **prayer**, O Lord, and give ear unto my **cry**."[9]
- "Evening, and morning, and at noon, will I **pray**, and **cry** aloud: and he shall hear my voice."[10]
- "Hear my **cry**, O God; attend unto my **prayer**."[11]
- "Hear my **prayer**, O Lord, and let my **cry** come unto thee. Hide not thy face from me in the day when I am in trouble; incline thine ear unto me: in the day when I **call** answer me speedily."[12]

Commands to Cry Out

Scripture gives several commands to cry out. A key passage is, "Call upon me in the day of trouble: I will deliver thee, and thou shalt glorify me."[13]

Two other passages give the same instruction and assurance that God will hear and respond. "The righteous cry, and the Lord heareth, and delivereth them out of all their troubles."[14] "When I cry unto thee, then shall mine enemies turn back: this I know; for God is for me."[15] A further Scripture on the importance of crying out is, "Call unto me, and I will answer thee, and shew thee great and mighty things, which thou knowest not."[16]

$Chapter\ 4$

Five Factors That Are Essential for Your Cry to Be Heard

There are specific factors that are necessary to make a cry effective. To the degree that these factors are missing, a cry loses its effectiveness and we do not experience the results that we are expecting.

If a baby whimpers while his father is working on a project, the father will probably finish his project and then attend to the needs of his baby. However, if the baby suddenly screams, the father will no doubt drop what he is doing, run over to his baby, and do whatever is necessary to resolve the problem.

God uses this very analogy to describe His care for His children. "Like as a father pitieth his children, so the LORD pitieth them that fear him. For he knoweth our frame; he remembereth that we are dust."[1] For a cry to be effective, it must reflect the qualities of a baby's cry.

1. Recognizing My Helplessness—
"I am unable to solve this problem."

An impossible crisis is usually necessary to bring us to the end of our self-confidence and self-effort. As long as we struggle to solve our problems, the Lord stands by and waits. His waiting should not seem unreasonable. Anyone who wants to rescue a drowning person is instructed to wait until the person stops struggling. Only then is the rescuer able to pull him to shore. This counsel has resulted from many rescuers being pulled underwater by the desperate struggles of the ones they are trying to save.

2. Conquering My Pride—
"I will humble myself and cry out for help."

The first time we cry out to God, we will experience a sense of humility that shatters a spirit of pride and self-sufficiency. A cry is an open declaration that we are incapable of dealing with a particular situation and that we are in desperate need of God's help.

A spirit of pride will keep us from crying out for help. We do not like to admit that we have a problem, much less to publicly acknowledge that we need outside help to resolve it. We want people to think that we are strong and self-sufficient.

"God resisteth the proud, but giveth grace unto the humble."[2] The first quality that Jesus taught His followers to cultivate was humility—to be "poor in spirit."[3] The Greek word He used describes a roadside beggar earnestly looking to others for daily provisions. Pride is wanting to be equal with God. It is believing that we have achieved what God and others have done for us and through us.

Many men believe that crying is a sign of weakness. Actually, the opposite is true. Jesus wept at the tomb of Lazarus, and He is not weak. After weeping, He used His power to raise Lazarus from the dead.[4]

3. Experiencing Hopelessness—
"No one but God can solve this problem."

When things look hopeless, we have the greatest possibility of God's intervention because He gets greater glory. It was hopeless for Abraham and Sarah to think of having a child. She was barren, and they were over ninety years old. Every other miracle in Scripture was based on the same sense of human hopelessness.

In Biblical times, the strength of an army was not primarily measured by the number of soldiers it had but by the number of horses and chariots. Iron chariots were particularly dreadful in battle.

It is therefore significant that God instructed His own people to not have horses or chariots. He knew how easy it would be for them to trust in these rather than looking to Him for victory. God is the One Who raises up armies and gives the battle to whom He will. The number of men and the amount of weapons have little to do with the outcome. "The horse is prepared against the day of battle: but safety is of the LORD."[5]

An example of God's response to a hopeless military situation took place when a great host from two enemy nations attacked Israel. Jehoshaphat the king "feared, and set himself to seek the LORD, and proclaimed a fast throughout all Judah."

Then he cried out, "O our God, wilt thou not judge them? for we have no might against this great company that cometh against us; neither know we what to do, but our eyes are upon thee."

The Lord answered with the message, "Be not afraid, nor dismayed by reason of this great multitude, for the battle is not yours, but God's."[6]

4. Surrendering Unconditionally—
"I will cleanse my life and fully obey God."

One of the major reasons that our cries are not effective is that we have idols in our hearts. An idol is anyone or anything that we look to for what only God can do. If, for example, we expect security from money, we make money an idol because only God can give us security. If we expect possessions or pleasures to fulfill us, we turn them into idols because we will experience fulfillment in life only by achieving the purposes for which God created us.

When the children of Israel cried out, God delivered them from their enemies, but then they began to forget God. They were soon overcome by other nations.

5. Expecting Results—
"I know that God can deliver me."

When the blind man cried out for Jesus to heal him, he fully expected that Jesus had the power to do it. This is true for every other person who cried out to the Lord and experienced His deliverance.

On that day when the crowd gathered along the road where Jesus would come, the blind man heard the commotion and then began to cry out, "Jesus, thou Son of David, have mercy on me." Bystanders told him to quiet down, but he cried even louder. He cried out because he knew that if Jesus heard him and received his request, he would be healed.[7]

This is the kind of faith that God looks for in every person who cries out to Him, for without this faith it is impossible to please God.[8] A powerful example of this kind of faith is seen in the following account.

"And a woman having an issue of blood twelve years, which had spent all her living upon physicians, neither could be healed of any, Came behind him, and touched the border of his garment: and immediately her issue of blood stanched. And Jesus said, Who touched me? When all denied, Peter and they that were with him said, Master, the multitude throng thee and press thee, and sayest thou, Who touched me?

"And Jesus said, Somebody hath touched me: for I perceive that virtue is gone out of me. And when the woman saw that she was not hid, she came trembling, and falling down before him, she declared unto him before all the people for what cause she had touched him, and how she was healed immediately. And he said unto her, Daughter, be of good comfort: thy faith hath made thee whole; go in peace."[9]

Chapter 5

Biblical Accounts That Demonstrate the Power of Crying Out

If the importance of an activity is determined by the number of different words that describe it, then crying out for God's deliverance is one of the most important activities in Scripture. There are about seventeen different Hebrew and Greek words that all mean the same thing—to cry out. The many different contexts in which these words are used illustrate the mighty power of God when they are acted upon.

Biblical Words for Crying Out

1. Tsa`aq—To cry out for help

"And the people murmured against Moses, saying, What shall we drink? And he **cried** [*tsa`aq*] unto the LORD; and the LORD shewed him a tree, which when he had cast into the waters, the waters were made sweet."[1]

2. Tas`aqah—A cry of deep distress

"The LORD also will be a refuge for the oppressed, a refuge in times of trouble. And they that know thy name will put their trust in thee: for thou, LORD, hast not forsaken them that seek thee. . . . When he maketh inquisition for blood, he remembereth them: he forgetteth not the **cry** [*tas`aqah*] of the humble. Have mercy upon me, O LORD; consider my trouble which I suffer of them that hate me."[2]

3. Za`aq—An outcry, cry of distress

Thou "didst see the affliction of our fathers in Egypt, and heardest their **cry** [za`aq] by the Red sea."[3]

4. Shav`ah—A cry for help

"He will fulfil the desire of them that fear him: he also will hear their **cry** [shav`ah], and will save them."[4]

5. Qara'—To call out with a loud sound

"The LORD is nigh unto all them that **call** [qara'] upon him, to all that **call** [qara'] upon him in truth."[5]

6. Rinnah—A ringing cry of entreaty

"Yet have thou respect unto the prayer of thy servant [Solomon], and to his supplication, O LORD my God, to hearken unto the **cry** [rinnah] and to the prayer, which thy servant prayeth before thee to-day."[6]

7. Ruwa`—To shout a war cry or an alarm

"And when Judah looked back, behold, the battle was before and behind: and they **cried** [tsa`aq] unto the LORD, and the priests sounded with the trumpets. Then the men of Judah gave a **shout** [ruwa`]: and as the men of Judah **shouted** [ruwa`], it came to pass, that God smote [their enemies]."[7]

8. Shava`—To cry out aloud and shout for help

"For he shall deliver the needy when he **crieth** [shava`]; the poor also, and him that hath no helper."[8]

9. Hamah—To cry out, to roar and be loud

"Evening, and morning, and at noon, will I pray, and **cry aloud** [hamah]: and he shall hear my voice."[9]

10. Tsahal—To cry aloud with shrillness

"**Cry out** [tsahal] and shout, thou inhabitant of Zion: for great is the Holy One of Israel in the midst of thee."[10]

11. Tsevachah—Outcry, shout

"Thy **cry** [*tsevachah*] hath filled the land: for the mighty man hath stumbled against the mighty, and they are fallen both together."[11]

12. Ranan—To give a ringing cry

"My soul longeth, yea, even fainteth for the courts of the LORD: my heart and my flesh **crieth out** [*ranan*] for the living God."[12]

13. 'Anaq—To cry and lament

"Thus saith the Lord GOD to Tyrus; Shall not the isles shake at the sound of thy fall, when the wounded **cry** [*'anaq*], when the slaughter is made in the midst of thee?"[13]

14. `Arag—To cry out and long for

"As the hart **panteth** [*`arag*] after the water brooks, so **panteth** [*`arag*] my soul after thee, O God."[14]

15. Kraugazo—To cry out

"And, behold, a woman of Canaan came out of the same coasts, and **cried** [*kraugazo*] unto him, saying, Have mercy on me, O Lord, thou son of David; my daughter is grievously vexed with a devil."[15]

"When he [Jesus] had offered up prayers and supplications with strong **crying** [*kraugazo*] and tears unto him that was able to save him from death, and was heard in that he feared."[16]

16. Krazo—To cry out

"And straightway the father of the child **cried out** [*krazo*], and said with tears, Lord, I believe; help thou mine unbelief."[17]

17. Boao—To cry out for help, to implore aid, to speak with a high, strong voice

"And shall not God avenge his own elect, which **cry** [*boao*] day and night unto him, though he bear long with them?"[18]

Biblical Examples of Crying Out

Freedom From the Bondage of Slavery

A widespread and prolonged famine in the Near East brought multitudes to the point of starvation. Meanwhile, the Pharaoh had an ample supply of corn because of following a wise plan that God had given to Joseph. The starving people were willing to sell whatever was necessary to buy food. Thus, it was not long before Pharaoh owned their herds, flocks, lands, and even the people themselves as servants.

After the famine, the Pharaoh maintained his absolute control over the people. He even relocated many to new cities. He also took advantage of a sentiment against the descendants of Abraham to launch ambitious building programs and use them as slave labor. This arrangement produced great wealth and power for the Pharaoh, which he was not about to surrender.

What, then, was the power that forced the Pharaoh to finally release over two million slaves who were essential to his economic prosperity? It was not an uprising of the slaves nor deliverance by a foreign army, but rather it was the fervent cry of those slaves to their God.

God said to Moses, "I have surely seen the affliction of my people which are in Egypt, and have heard their cry by reason of their taskmasters; for I know their sorrows; And I am come down to deliver them out of the hand of the Egyptians."[19]

Protection From a Pursuing Army

When Pharaoh realized the financial, political, and social impact of releasing his slaves, he ordered his army to pursue them. The army encountered the former slaves at the edge of the Red Sea. It would be an easy matter to round them up and force them back to Egypt. The Israelites were especially fearful of Pharaoh's horses and chariots. When they saw that they were trapped, they cried out to God for deliverance. "When Pharaoh drew nigh, the children of Israel lifted up their eyes, and, behold, the Egyptians marched after them;

and they were sore afraid: and the children of Israel cried out unto the LORD."[20]

God's supernatural response to their cries is a marvel of history. He opened up the sea with a wind so that the nation walked across on dry land. When the army of Egypt pursued, the waters returned and they were drowned.

Provision for Hunger and Thirst in the Wilderness

After crossing the Red Sea, the nation of Israel faced a new threat to their existence—starvation. How could over two million people find food and water in the barren wilderness of the Sinai Desert? They cried out to the Lord. "They wandered in the wilderness in a solitary way; they found no city to dwell in. Hungry and thirsty, their soul fainted in them. Then they cried unto the LORD in their trouble, and he delivered them out of their distresses."[21]

Deliverance From Attacking Armies of Greater Strength

At every turn, the nation of Israel faced impossible circumstances for survival. They encountered insurmountable obstacles and well-armed enemies. Yet, whenever they cried out, God delivered them.

"And they were helped against them, and the Hagarites were delivered into their hand, and all that were with them: for they cried to God in the battle, and he was entreated of them; because they put their trust in him."[22]

The children of Israel cried out to God when they were in desperate perils. However, when the danger was passed and prosperity experienced, the nations became comfortable and self-reliant. They began to attribute their health, wealth, and safety to other causes and ceased to worship the God of their forefathers. God had chosen this nation to be an example to all other nations of what He would do for the people who were in fellowship with Him and followed His ways. It was a particular concern, therefore, when the people turned from Him to serve other gods.

"And they cried unto the LORD, and said, We have sinned, because we have forsaken the LORD, and have served Baalim and Ashtaroth: but now deliver us out of the hand of our enemies, and we will serve thee. And the LORD sent Jerubbaal, and Bedan, and Jephthah, and Samuel, and delivered you out of the hand of your enemies on every side, and ye dwelled safe."[23]

When the ten northern tribes of Israel turned away from the Lord to serve other gods, a civil war erupted. The tribe of Judah that remained faithful to God cried out in the battle and experienced God's deliverance.

"And when Judah looked back, behold, the battle was before and behind: and they cried unto the LORD, and the priests sounded with the trumpets. Then the men of Judah gave a shout: and as the men of Judah shouted, it came to pass, that God smote Jeroboam and all Israel before Abijah and Judah. . . . and the children of Judah prevailed, because they relied upon the LORD God of their fathers."[24]

Individuals Who Experienced God's Power by Crying Out

In addition to hearing the cries of groups, God delights in showing Himself strong through the cries of anyone who is facing an impossible situation and who will cry out for His deliverance.

Jehoshaphat Cried Out in the Face of Death

"And it came to pass, when the captains of the chariots saw Jehoshaphat, that they said, It is the king of Israel. Therefore they compassed about him to fight: but Jehoshaphat **cried out**, and the LORD helped him; and God moved them to depart from him."[25]

David Cried Out in the Midst of Troubles

"This poor man **cried**, and the LORD heard him, and saved him out of all his troubles."[26] "In the day when I cried thou answeredst me, and strengthenedst me with strength in my soul."[27]

A Troubled Father Cried Out for His Son

"Jesus said unto him, If thou canst believe, all things are possible to him that believeth. And straightway the father of the child **cried out**, and said with tears, Lord, I believe; help thou mine unbelief."[28]

A Mother Cried Out for Her Afflicted Daughter

"And, behold, a woman of Canaan came out of the same coasts, and **cried** unto him, saying, Have mercy on me, O Lord, thou son of David; my daughter is grievously vexed with a devil. But he answered her not a word. And his disciples came and besought him, saying, Send her away, for she crieth after us. But he answered and said, I am not sent but unto the lost sheep of the house of Israel. Then came she and worshipped him, saying, Lord, help me. But he answered and said, It is not meet to take the children's bread, and cast it to the dogs. And she said, Truth, Lord: yet the dogs eat of the crumbs which fall from their masters' table. Then Jesus answered and said unto her, O woman, great is thy faith: be it unto thee even as thou wilt. And her daughter was made whole from that very hour."[29]

Elijah Cried Out for the Son of a Widow

"And he **cried** unto the LORD, and said, O LORD my God, hast thou also brought evil upon the widow with whom I sojourn, by slaying her son? And he stretched himself upon the child three times, and **cried** unto the LORD, and said, O LORD my God, I pray thee, let this child's soul come into him again. And the LORD heard the voice of Elijah; and the soul of the child came into him again, and he revived."[30]

Peter Cried Out in a Stormy Sea

"But when he saw the wind boisterous, he was afraid; and beginning to sink, he **cried**, saying, Lord, save me. And immediately Jesus stretched forth his hand, and caught him."[31]

The Blind Man Cried Out for Sight

"And he **cried**, saying, Jesus, thou son of David, have mercy on me. And they which went before rebuked him, that he should hold his peace: but he **cried** so much the more, Thou son of David, have mercy on me. And Jesus stood, and commanded him to be brought unto him: and when he was come near, he asked him, Saying, What wilt thou that I shall do unto thee? And he said, Lord, that I may receive my sight. And Jesus said unto him, Receive thy sight: thy faith hath saved thee. And immediately he received his sight, and followed him, glorifying God: and all the people, when they saw it, gave praise unto God."[32]

Chapter 6

The Most Important Cry
You Will Ever Make

The one relationship in life that is more important than
any other is our relationship with God. How, then, do we
establish fellowship with Him? It is interesting that Scripture
does not speak of establishing this relationship with a prayer,
but rather with a cry.

Notice how references in both the Old and New Testaments
explain that salvation comes through a cry. On the Day of
Pentecost, Peter spoke to the multitudes about their personal
guilt. When they asked what they must do, he answered,
"Whosoever shall **call** on the name of the Lord shall be
saved."[1] The Greek word that Peter used is *epikaleomai*, mean-
ing "to call upon for one's self."

Peter was actually quoting a verse from the Book of Joel,
which he said was being fulfilled that very day. The verse is,
"And it shall come to pass, that whosoever shall **call** on the
name of the LORD shall be delivered."[2] The word *call* in this
passage is the Hebrew word *qara'*, which means "to cry out."

The Apostle Paul confirmed that crying out to God
brings salvation. "That if thou shalt confess with thy mouth
the Lord Jesus, and shalt believe in thine heart that God hath
raised him from the dead, thou shalt be saved. For with the
heart man believeth unto righteousness; and with the mouth
confession is made unto salvation. For the scripture saith,
Whosoever believeth on him shall not be ashamed. For there

is no difference between the Jew and the Greek: for the same Lord over all is rich unto all that **call** upon him. For whosoever shall **call** upon the name of the Lord shall be saved."[3]

When Paul wrote to the believers in the Corinthian church, he addressed his letter to "them that are sanctified in Christ Jesus, called to be saints, with all that in every place **call** upon the name of Jesus Christ our Lord."[4] David also speaks of receiving salvation by crying out to the Lord. "I will take the cup of salvation, and **call** upon the name of the LORD."[5]

In the parable of the Pharisee and the publican going to the Temple, the Pharisee prayed with himself and rehearsed the good things he had done for God. "God, I thank thee, that I am not as other men are, extortioners, unjust, adulterers, or even as this publican. I fast twice in the week, I give tithes of all that I possess."[6]

The publican, on the other hand, was so convicted of his sinful condition that he did not even look up, but he smote his chest and cried out, "God be merciful to me a sinner." Jesus said, "I tell you, this man went down to his house justified rather than the other: for every one that exalteth himself shall be abased; and he that humbleth himself shall be exalted."[7]

Two men were crucified with Jesus Christ. One railed against Him, but the other cried out, "Lord, remember me when thou comest into thy kingdom!" Jesus said to him, "Today thou shalt be with me in paradise."[8]

This Is a Cry With No Prerequisites

Anyone who cries out for God's mercy in salvation will be given that mercy and salvation by the Lord. This is the promise in the verse, "Whosoever shall call on the name of the Lord shall be saved."[9] Those who call upon the Lord are instantly born again by the Spirit of God. The Spirit of God then dwells within that person and energizes him or her to cry out for further needs.

$Chapter\ 7$

Seven Reasons Why God
May Not Hear a Cry

God will hear anyone's prayer for salvation. However, if the following factors are in our lives, He may not hear our cries in other matters.

1. Not crying out with the whole heart

God heard the cries of David because David cried out with his whole heart. He wrote, "I cried with my whole heart; hear me, O LORD: I will keep thy statutes."[1]

God is looking for those whose hearts are pure so that He can show His power through them, "For the eyes of the LORD run to and fro throughout the whole earth, to shew himself strong in the behalf of them whose heart is perfect toward him."[2]

In contrast to David's integrity, the people of Hosea's time did not cry out with their whole hearts and, therefore, God did not respond to them. "And they have not cried unto me with their heart, when they howled upon their beds: they assemble themselves for corn and wine, and they rebel against me."[3]

2. Not crying out with genuine humility

The very act of crying out is a humbling experience, yet pride is like a cancer in our hearts and only removing part of it multiplies the problem. Pride is in total and direct opposition to God and to all that He wants to do in and through our lives. God promises to hear the cry of the humble: "He forgetteth not the cry of the humble."[4]

The very nature of a cry is to humble one's self and to give unconditional surrender to God and His will. Pride is reserving to ourselves the right to make final decisions. Humility is turning that right over to God with no strings attached. Pride is building life around ourselves. Humility is relating our lives around God and the needs of others. Pride is being concerned about my reputation and how other people think of us. Humility is being more concerned about what God thinks of us because He is the One Who determines whether we are exalted or abased. "God is the judge: he putteth down one, and setteth up another."[5]

Pride is the worst of all sins because it is our attempt to be equal with God. Therefore, He judges it quickly and severely. When Lucifer, who is now Satan, stated, "I will be like the most high," he was cast out of heaven, along with the third of the angels who rebelled with him. Satan then tempted Eve with a similar appeal. "If you partake of the forbidden fruit, you will be like gods." Humility does not consist of thinking less of ourselves; it is simply not thinking of ourselves.

3. Not crying out with the voice

It is possible to pray in our hearts without making any sound with our lips, but it is not possible to cry out without using the voice. When Hannah was asking for a son, the Scripture says, "She spake in her heart; only her lips moved, but her voice was not heard."[6] God heard her prayer and answered it. On the other hand, David made it clear that when he cried, he did it with his voice. "Evening, and morning, and at noon, will I pray, and cry aloud: and he shall hear my voice."[7] David further states, "I cried unto the LORD with my voice; with my voice unto the LORD did I make my supplication."[8]

Even Jonah managed to cry out with his voice in the belly of the great fish. "I cried by reason of mine affliction unto the LORD, and he heard me; out of the belly of hell cried I, and thou heardest my voice."[9]

4. Not being sincere when we repent

David states that he cried unto the Lord with his mouth and his tongue, but then he reminds himself, "If I regard iniquity in my heart, the Lord will not hear me."[10] Iniquity is simply doing my own will, even though it looks good to others. Jesus did nothing of His own will, but only the will of His heavenly Father. It is often our self-will that gets us into trouble and brings us to the place of needing to cry out to God.

"Behold, the Lord's hand is not shortened, that it cannot save; neither his ear heavy, that it cannot hear: But your iniquities have separated between you and your God, and your sins have hid his face from you, that he will not hear."[11]

A father may have a strong desire to help other people and yet neglect his own family. When his own wife or children begin to rebel, he may cry out to God for help and wonder why his cry is not being heard. It would be wise for him to stop crying out and search the Scriptures, which will instruct him to first go to those whom he has offended and make things right with them.[12]

When we repent of the things that displease God, He will deliver us from our troubles. But if we continue to go back to sinful ways, we may find ourselves in the position of the children of Israel when they "cried unto the LORD, saying, We have sinned against thee, both because we have forsaken our God, and also served Baalim."[13]

This repentance sounds sincere, yet God reminded them of the following. "Did not I deliver you from the Egyptians, and from the Amorites, from the children of Ammon, and from the Philistines? The Zidonians also, and the Amalekites, and the Maonites, did oppress you; and ye cried to me, and I delivered you out of their hand. Yet ye have forsaken me, and served other gods: wherefore I will deliver you no more. Go and cry unto the gods which ye have chosen; let them deliver you in the time of your tribulation."[14]

5. Not fulfilling past vows

Making a vow to God is a very serious matter because there are severe consequences for breaking a vow. Thus we are warned, "When thou vowest a vow unto God, defer not to pay it; for he hath no pleasure in fools: pay that which thou hast vowed. Better is it that thou shouldest not vow, than that thou shouldest vow and not pay. Suffer not thy mouth to cause thy flesh to sin; neither say thou before the angel, that it was an error: wherefore should God be angry at thy voice, and destroy the work of thine hands?"[15]

A major verse of promise on crying out is, "And call upon me in the day of trouble: I will deliver thee, and thou shalt glorify me."[16] It is significant that the verse that precedes this reads as follows: "Offer unto God thanksgiving; and pay thy vows unto the most High."[17]

There is specific reference in Scripture to those who cry out but are not heard because they have been unfaithful to marriage vows. "And this have ye done again, covering the altar of the LORD with tears, with weeping, and with crying out, insomuch that he regardeth not the offering any more, or receiveth it with good will at your hand. Yet ye say, Wherefore? Because the LORD hath been witness between thee and the wife of thy youth, against whom thou hast dealt treacherously: yet is she thy companion, and the wife of thy covenant. And did not he make one? Yet had he the residue of the spirit. And wherefore one? That he might seek a godly seed. Therefore take heed to your spirit, and let none deal treacherously against the wife of his youth."[18]

David committed adultery with Bathsheba and then tried to cover it up by arranging the death of her husband. He cried out in repentance and God forgave him. However, he told David that because he had sinned, there would be continual trouble in his own household. When further trials and disasters came to David, he reminded himself that they were caused by his sin, and the theme of his life became the mercy of the Lord.

6. Not giving to the needs of the poor

God has a special concern for four groups of people: the fatherless, the widows, the strangers (foreigners), and the poor. Those in these groups often have special needs and crises that others do not experience, and God's ear is open to their cries. God also expects us to respond to their cries and do what we can to assist them. Our failure to do this is observed and remembered by the Lord. "Whoso stoppeth his ears at the cry of the poor, he also shall cry himself, but shall not be heard."[19]

Even more serious consequences will come to anyone who oppresses those in these groups and causeth them to cry out for God's help. "Ye shall not afflict any widow, or fatherless child. If thou afflict them in any wise, and they cry at all unto me, I will surely hear their cry; And my wrath shall wax hot, and I will kill you with the sword; and your wives shall be widows, and your children fatherless."[20]

God will also punish the employer who does not give to his employees that which is just and agreed upon. "Thou shalt not oppress an hired servant that is poor and needy, whether he be of thy brethren, or of thy strangers that are in thy land within thy gates: At his day thou shalt give him his hire, neither shall the sun go down upon it; for he is poor, and setteth his heart upon it: lest he cry against thee unto the LORD, and it be sin unto thee."[21]

7. Not resolving anger and bitterness

God warns husbands not to be bitter toward their wives but to dwell with their wives according to knowledge, so their prayers will not be hindered.[22] If their prayers are hindered, their cries will also be ineffective. God gives each one of us the ability to respond to the hurts of life through His grace. We are to be careful that no one resists that grace; otherwise, a root of bitterness will spring up, and by this means many people have been defiled. Scripture relates this defilement to problems that Esau had when he cried out for a blessing and was rejected.[23]

The story of Hagar provides a beautiful picture of offenses, reactions, crying out, and God's responses. When Hagar despised Sarai (Sarah) in her heart, a conflict arose between them, and Hagar fled to the wilderness. The angel of the Lord told her to return and submit to Sarah's leadership. He also instructed her to name her unborn child Ishmael, which means "God hears." Years later, Hagar was sent away with Ishmael to the wilderness. Both cried out to the Lord. "And God heard the voice of the lad; and the angel of God called to Hagar out of heaven, and said unto her, What aileth thee, Hagar? fear not; for God hath heard the voice of the lad where he is."[24]

Chapter 8

Why the "Prayer" of Jabez Is So Effective

Millions of people are now using the prayer of Jabez on a daily basis. Their inspiration for doing this has not only come from the book written by Dr. Bruce Wilkinson entitled *The Prayer of Jabez*, but from the amazing results that so many are experiencing from it. In the first year and a half since its publication, it has sold over 8.6 million copies. For twenty-five weeks, it has been on the *New York Times* best-seller list.

The prayer of Jabez is powerful because it is actually a cry and not just a prayer. Scripture states, "And Jabez called on the God of Israel."[1] In this verse, the Hebrew word for *called* is *qara'*. It means, "to call out with a loud sound."

What Motivated Jabez to Cry Out?

Jabez had seven older brothers. He was the last child born to a mother who named him Jabez because she bore him "with sorrow."[2] We learn from the history of the Jewish nation what caused her sorrow. After Jabez was conceived, her husband died. Thus, Jabez was born fatherless to a grieving, widowed mother.

She might also have been grieving over another family matter. Her seven older sons decided that they did not want to share their father's inheritance with Jabez. Therefore, before he was born, they divided the inheritance into seven parts. As Jabez grew up, he realized that there would be no father to bless him and no inheritance waiting for him. Rather than becoming bitter, he sought the Lord and looked to Him for blessing.

When Jabez reached the age of thirteen, he went through the ceremony of bar mitzvah, which is the passage from childhood to adulthood. At that time, he cried out, "Oh that thou wouldest bless me indeed, and enlarge my coast, and that thine hand might be with me, and that thou wouldest keep me from evil, that it may not grieve me!"[3]

The spiritual leaders who heard this cry and observed the life of young Jabez were so impressed with his spiritual maturity and understanding of his heavenly Father that they came to him for counsel. Eventually, he began a school to train spiritual leaders. It was called the School of Jabez. As additional land was required for Jabez's ministry, it was secured and soon there was a city. The only other reference to Jabez in Scripture refers to families of the scribes who lived in the city of Jabez.[4]

Scripture states that "Jabez was more honourable than his brethren."[5] When he cried out for God to bless him and enlarge his coast, he was not desiring a selfish benefit, but the ability to enlarge his ministry with whatever land was necessary.

How Should We Apply the Cry of Jabez?

It is certainly proper to ask God to bless us. Jacob wrestled with the angel and said, "I will not let thee go, except thou bless me."[6] At that point, God blessed Jacob and changed his name from Jacob to Israel because he had power with God. It is the name of Israel that Jabez used for his appeal. "Jabez called on the God of Israel."[7]

However, when David cried out to the Lord for a blessing, he used the word *us* rather than *me*: "God be merciful unto us, and bless us."[8] When Jesus taught His disciples to pray, He did not tell us to pray "my father, " but rather "our father." "Our Father. . . . Give us this day our daily bread. . . . lead us not into temptation, but deliver us from evil."[9]

Whether we pray "bless me" or "bless us," we should always keep in mind that we are in a covenant with all the members of the Body of Christ. Thus, when one member is blessed, all the members are benefited.[10]

How a Cry Enlarged a Coast for Ministry

ALERT is a branch of the Institute ministry that responds to emergencies such as tornadoes, hurricanes, floods, fires, and terrorist bombings. Since its beginning in 1994, hundreds of young men have been trained in character and emergency skills through this program at our Northwoods Training Center.

After several years, the facilities were being used to their capacity. The program's founder's wife began to cry out to the Lord with the prayer of Jabez, and a staff member was dispatched to find a larger facility. He returned with a beautifully illustrated booklet describing a fabulous 2,200-acre university campus.

The campus area contained over one hundred buildings, including attractively furnished dorms, administrative buildings, and a spacious gymnasium and dining area. The complex had a one-mile airstrip, a 1,000-acre farm, an 800-acre pine forest, a 220-acre equipped recreational vehicle park, two lakes surrounded by seventeen staff homes, a library of 130,000 volumes, a radio station, and many other features.

This was a "coast" larger than we ever imagined! So was the asking price! Since the beginning of the Institute ministry in 1961, the Lord has directed us not to ask people for funds or to borrow any money. Therefore, we prayed that God would provide for this need.

A few months later, we experienced a "death" to our vision. Another organization signed a contract to purchase this property.

Almost three years later, the broker who handled this property called and informed us that the other organization was not able to come up with the money. He then asked if we were still interested in buying it. We assured him that we were, but we did not have the funds they were requesting for the property. He responded by saying, "Make us an offer!"

This was the rebirth of a vision. In the intervening years, two different groups had expressed an interest in supporting the Institute by sponsoring a larger project. However, this project was even bigger than their intentions. After seeing the property, they made a combined offer, which we presented to the sellers. To our amazement, they accepted it.

It took longer than expected to work out the contract, but finally it was done. Then we received an urgent e-mail from the sellers telling us not to sign it because they had received another offer millions of dollars higher than ours.

Our hearts sank. This was "double death" to our vision. We experienced deep anguish of soul as we realized the extent of our loss. Not only would we lose the use of the campus with its facilities, but also the millions of dollars that had been designated just for that project.

In the midst of our distress and realization of our impossible situation, we had only one recourse—cry out to the Lord. Several of us got on our knees and in a loud voice cried out, "O Lord, Abba, Father, deliver this property for your work!"

As soon as we made that cry, three words came to my mind. The words were, "Write a letter." I thought, "What good would a letter do to counteract a higher offer of millions of dollars?" Yet the thought persisted, so we sat down and wrote a 1½-page letter.

It was e-mailed to the sellers. Several hours later, we received a phone call from the sellers. They informed us that they had read our letter, and on the basis of what we had written, they had decided to sell us the property if we could complete the transaction by Friday afternoon at five o'clock. This condition was met after several more times of crying out. At 4:55 Friday afternoon, the title was transferred!

Chapter 9

How to Thank God for Hearing and Answering Our Cries

There are several important factors that all of us need to remember in the matter of crying out.

1. Realize the futility of our own efforts.

Trying to live out the Christian life by our own strength is impossible. This fact will be confirmed by a quick review of New Testament commands: Let all anger be put away from you,[1] love your enemies and do good to those who hate you,[2] be perfect,[3] be holy,[4] pray without ceasing,[5] love God with all your heart and all your soul and all your mind and your neighbor as yourself.[6]

2. Humble ourselves daily.

One day, I urged a teenager who had been entrusted to us from a Florida juvenile court to decide that he would obey a certain command of Scripture. He said, "No." However, when I asked him why he would not make this commitment, he gave me a very good answer: "Because I know I could not keep my commitment."

He was right. It is only by abiding in the Lord Jesus Christ and by the grace of God that we have the desire or power to do God's will. I remembered the promise that God resists the proud but gives grace to the humble, so I asked him if he would be willing to find ways each day to humble himself so that God would give him the grace to carry out this commitment.

He was willing to do this. In fact, we both got on our knees and told God that each day we would look for ways to humble ourselves before Him.

Since that day, I have begun each day by getting on my face before God and acknowledging my total unworthiness and inability to do anything for Him. I then ask Him to work in and through me. Scripture states: "Humble yourselves therefore under the mighty hand of God, that he may exalt you in due time."[7] I have learned by painful experience that if I do not humble myself, God has many others who will "volunteer" to do it for me.

3. Remember why God creates crises.

The crises of life are designed by God to remind us of our human weakness and His divine power. He wants us to cry out to Him for His supernatural work. As we call upon Him, He has promised to deliver us. He has also promised to show us great and mighty things.[8]

God's purpose in doing all this is clearly stated in the words, "Call upon me in the day of trouble: I will deliver thee, and thou shalt glorify me."[9] This same goal is further explained in the passage that speaks of God's mighty deliverance from the storms that brought people to their "wits' end." "Then they cried unto the LORD in their trouble, and he delivered them out of their distresses."[10]

4. Tell others of God's powerful acts.

Since God's ultimate purpose in all His creation is to demonstrate the glory of His love and power, we fulfill that purpose by telling others of His mighty works in our lives. Scripture states, "Let the redeemed of the LORD say so, whom he hath redeemed from the hand of the enemy."[11] David wrote, "Oh that men would praise the LORD for his goodness, and for his wonderful works to the children of men! Let them exalt him also in the congregation of the people, and praise him in the assembly of the elders."[12]

As we cry out to God and He answers us, let's look for ways to share the results with others. A special Web site is being prepared so that we can report to the world the mighty power of God in the lives of those who cry out to Him. E-mail your report to powerfulcries@iblp.org.

Endnotes

Introduction
1. Jeremiah 33:3.

Chapter 1
1. Psalm 50:15.
2. Psalm 50:15.
3. Ephesians 6:12.
4. Proverbs 16:6.

Chapter 2
1. See Matthew 8:23–26;
   Luke 8:22–25.
2. Matthew 10:36.
3. Psalm 55:12–14.
4. II Corinthians 12:10.
5. Luke 18:4–8.
6. Psalm 107:23–24.
7. Psalm 50:15.

Chapter 3
1. Matthew 26:40–41.
2. James 5:17–18.
3. James 5:16.
4. Colossians 1:29.
5. Acts 4:31.
6. See Acts 2:1, 46; 4:24;
   5:12.
7. Acts 2:42.
8. Psalm 17:1.
9. Psalm 39:12.
10. Psalm 55:17.
11. Psalm 61:1.
12. Psalm 102:1–2.
13. Psalm 50:15.
14. Psalm 34:17.
15. Psalm 56:9.
16. Jeremiah 33:3.

Chapter 4
1. Psalm 103:13–14.
2. James 4:6.
3. Matthew 5:3.
4. See John 11:35.
5. Proverbs 21:31.
6. See II Chronicles
   20:1–24.
7. See Mark 10:46–52.
8. See Hebrews 11:6.
9. Luke 8:43–48.

Chapter 5
1. Exodus 15:24–25.
2. Psalm 9:9–13.
3. Nehemiah 9:9.
4. Psalm 145:19.
5. Psalm 145:18.
6. I Kings 8:28.
7. II Chronicles 13:14–15.
8. Psalm 72:12.
9. Psalm 55:17.
10. Isaiah 12:6.
11. Jeremiah 46:12.
12. Psalm 84:2.
13. Ezekiel 26:15.
14. Psalm 42:1.
15. Matthew 15:22.
16. Hebrews 5:7.
17. Mark 9:24.
18. Luke 18:7.
19. Exodus 3:7–8.
20. Exodus 14:10.
21. Psalm 107:4–6.
22. I Chronicles 5:20.
23. I Samuel 12:10–11.
24. II Chronicles 13:14–18.
25. II Chronicles 18:31.
26. Psalm 34:6.
27. Psalm 138:3.
28. Mark 9:23–24.
29. Matthew 15:22–28.
30. I Kings 17:20–22.
31. Matthew 14:30–31.
32. Luke 18:38–43.

Chapter 6
1. Acts 2:21.
2. Joel 2:32.
3. Romans 10:9–13.
4. I Corinthians 1:2.
5. Psalm 116:13.
6. Luke 18:11–12.
7. See Luke 18:13–14.
8. Luke 23:42–43.
9. Acts 2:21.

Chapter 7
1. Psalm 119:45.
2. II Chronicles 16:9.
3. Hosea 7:14.
4. Psalm 9:12.
5. Psalm 75:7.

6. I Samuel 1:13.
7. Psalm 55:17.
8. Psalm 142:1.
9. Jonah 2:2.
10. Palm 66:17.
11. Isaiah 59:1–2.
12. See Matthew 5:23–24;
    I Timothy 1:19.
13. Judges 10:10.
14. Judges 10:11–14.
15. Ecclesiastes 5:4–6.
16. Psalm 50:15.
17. Psalm 50:14.
18. Malachi 2:13–15.
19. Proverbs 21:13.
20. Exodus 22:22–24.
21. Deuteronomy 24:14–15.
22. See Colossians 3:19;
    I Peter 3:7.
23. See Hebrews 12:15–17.
24. Genesis 21:17.

Chapter 8
1. I Chronicles 4:10.
2. See I Chronicles 4:9.
3. I Chronicles 4:10.
4. See I Chronicles 2:55.
5. I Chronicles 4:9.
6. Genesis 32:26.
7. I Chronicles 4:10.
8. Psalm 67:1.
9. Matthew 6:9–13.
10. See I Corinthians 12:26.

Chapter 9
1. See Ephesians 4:31.
2. See Luke 6:27.
3. II Corinthians 13:11.
4. See I Peter 1:16.
5. I Thessalonians 5:17.
6. See Luke 10:27.
7. I Peter 5:6.
8. See Jeremiah 33:3.
9. Psalm 50:15.
10. Psalm 107:6.
11. Psalm 107:2.
12. Psalm 107:31–32.

My Experience of Crying Out

My Impossible Situation (go ahead and try it):

_____

_____

_____

_____

_____

_____

_____

_____

How I Cried Out (words and date):

_____

_____

_____

How God Delivered (it won't happen until you cry out):

_____

_____

_____

_____

_____

_____

_____

My Experience of Crying Out

My Impossible Situation (go ahead and try it):

_____

_____

_____

_____

_____

_____

_____

_____

How I Cried Out (words and date):

_____

_____

_____

How God Delivered (it won't happen until you cry out):

_____

_____

_____

_____

_____

_____

_____

My Experience of Crying Out

My Impossible Situation (go ahead and try it):

_____
_____
_____
_____
_____
_____
_____
_____

How I Cried Out (words and date):

_____
_____
_____

How God Delivered (it won't happen until you cry out):

_____
_____
_____
_____
_____
_____

My Experience of Crying Out

My Impossible Situation (go ahead and try it):

_____

_____

_____

_____

_____

_____

_____

_____

_____

How I Cried Out (words and date):

_____

_____

_____

_____

How God Delivered (it won't happen until you cry out):

_____

_____

_____

_____

_____

_____

_____

My Experience of Crying Out

My Impossible Situation (go ahead and try it):

_____

_____

_____

_____

_____

_____

_____

_____

How I Cried Out (words and date):

_____

_____

_____

How God Delivered (it won't happen until you cry out):

_____

_____

_____

_____

_____

_____

_____